1. **PREFACE**

This book contains the new bor.. quotations
or statements based on good observations
and are related to human activities
.Quotations say many a things at a glance.
Which line can change your life is unknown
to all. It has been seen that one or two lines
statement has changed the life to many
persons. It has revolutionized the career.
This book is most suitable in the following
activities-

to speak publically

to describe an event

to write something

to develop your personality

to think positive and feel energetic.

It is also helpful to all students from 8th
class to university level. These quotations
will give you energy to go ahead.

2.Contents

You biggest mistakes will lead to
your biggest learning opportunities.
--Wakil Kumar Yadav

If u teach mental toughness but
ignore the spiritual battle between
fear & faith that every human
experiences you're missing the mark.
--Wakil Kumar Yadav

Whatever is bringing down let it go!
U don't need that negativity in Ur
life. Keep calm & be positive. Good
things will happen.
--Wakil Kumar Yadav

 its funny how u can do nice things
for people all the time & they never
notice. But once u make one mistake,
it's never forgotten.
-Wakil Kumar Yadav

 Life becomes more meaningful
when u realizes the simple fact that
you'll never get the same moment
twice.
-Wakil Kumar Yadav

 Fast food restaurants use yellow,
red, & orange because those are the
colors that stimulate hunger.

3

If you are criticized by people, it means u are special to them.
-Wakil Kumar Yadav
some little achievements forces to forget the world for someone but not all.

Some people become blind after achieving something while some people become polite after achieving many things.
-Wakil kumar yadav

A Foolish thinks everything while fooling you so one should think everything to get rid of it.
-Wakil Kumar Yadav
Anti-elements always try to insult you either you do right or wrong, so never expect anything from them.
-Wakil Kumar Yadav
Human sounds a time but insects sounds all the time.
-Wakil Kumar Yadav
Laziness biggest laziness
-Wakil kumar yadav
Diamonds are not accessible to every hand but iron accessible to every hand.
-Wakil Kumar Yadav

If an egg is broken by outside force life ends. If an egg is broken by inside force, life begins. Great things always begin from inside.
--*Wakil Kumar Yadav*

The biggest prison people live is in the fear of what others thing.
--*Wakil Kumar Yadav*

Be with someone who will take care of u. Not materialistically, but takes care of Ur soul, Ur well being, Ur heart & everything that's u.
--*Wakil Kumar Yadav*

If we clean everything outside while poisoning minds with hatred, will we achieve Swachh Bharat??
--*Wakil Kumar Yadav*

: its ok and "I'm fine" are the two most common lies spoken in the world.
--*Wakil Kumar Yadav*

There are no such things as "I don't have time"- you just simply need to prioritize better.
--*Wakil Kumar Yadav*

Don't broadcast every high & low of Ur life. Just live. Don't try to

convince the world u have a life.
    --Wakil Kumar Yadav

If your mostly activities match to
common people
it means you are also a common
man,
if your mostly activities match to the
special people then you are special to
them.
-Wakil Kumar Yadav

Acquire such knowledge so you
don't need for others opinion.
-Wakil Kumar Yadav
Life & death r so unpredictable .So
close to each other. We exist
moment to moment, never knowing
who would be the next to leave the
world.
Wakil Kumar Yadav
Justice Dies when rapists are
supported
by the people.
Wakil Kumar Yadav
Even a tree that remains rooted in
one place eventually becomes a
landmark.

6

Wakil Kumar Yadav
Light always finds a way to shine.
Wakil Kumar Yadav
The pain which does not flow with
tears,
often found on paper with scatter
words.
Wakil Kumar Yadav
"The whole problem with the world
is that fools and fanatics are always
so certain of themselves, and wiser
people so full of doubts."
Wakil Kumar Yadav

"Victory goes to the player who
makes the next-to-last mistake."
Wakil Kumar Yadav
**"One day it just clicks.
You realize
what's important and what
isn't.
You learn to care less about
what other people think of you
and more about
what you think of yourself.
You realize how far you've
come
and you remember
when you thought
things were such a mess**

7

that you would never
recover.
And you smile.
You smile because you are
truly proud of yourself
and the person
you've fought to become."
~ Wakil Kumar Yadav
"Don't audit life.
Show up and make
the most of it now."
~ Wakil Kumar Yadav
"Arguing with an idiot is like
playing chess with a pigeon.
No matter how good you are,
the bird is going to poop on
the board
and strut around as if it won."
~ Wakil Kumar Yadav
"Worrying won't stop
the bad stuff from happening.
It just stops
you from enjoying the good."
~ Wakil Kumar Yadav
Don't wrestle a pig
both will get dirty
but the pig will enjoy it.
Wakil Kumar Yadav
Avoid ruffians all the time
because they are not born to be
changed.
Wakil Kumar Yadav
Villagers are rich by the heart

8

but cities are rich by wealth.
Wakil kumar yadav

Always be thankful for the bad
things in life. They open Ur eyes to
see the good things u weren't paying
attention to before.
--Wakil Kumar Yadav

Our brains have a negativity bias and
will remember negative memories
more than good ones. This helps us
to better protect ourselves.

--Wakil Kumar Yadav

When everything seems to be going
against u, remember that the airplane
takes off against the wind, not worth
it.
    --Wakil Kumar Yadav

People tend to find explanations that

include references to the brain very
convincing, even if those references
are mostly nonsense.

--Wakil Kumar Yadav

In you've got to get up every
morning with determination if you're
going to go to bed with satisfaction.

--Wakil Kumar Yadav

Humans have a strong relationship
with music bcoz of the way that
music affects our feelings, our
thinking & our emotional state.

--Wakil Kumar Yadav
Although we may find comfort in
speech, silence may also have some
virtue.
Wakil Kumar Yadav
Promise is a big word.
It either makes something
or it breaks everything".
Wakil Kumar Yadav
Helping others is a nice way to help
you.
Wakil Kumar Yadav
No summit of achievement is
attained in solo endeavors.
-Wakil Kumar Yadav
Ask the soul

10

SOLITUDE IS AN ACHIEVEMENT.
Life does not need to be perfect to
be wonderful.
Wakil Kumar Yadav
The future belongs to those who
believe
in the beauty of their dreams.
Wakil Kumar Yadav
Even a tree that remains rooted in
one place eventually becomes a
landmark...
Wakil Kumar Yadav

Greatness is never built with fear,
ego & division.
Greatness is always built with love,
sacrifice & unity.
Wakil Kumar Yadav

Curiosity is the most elegant

excuse for paying attention.
Wakil Kumar Yadav
A journey of a thousand memories
begins with a single step.
Wakil Kumar Yadav
CLARIFIES THE STEPS TO SIMPLIFY
THE JOURNEY.
Wakil Kumar Yadav
Ignoring the truth keeps you

in the shadows.
Wakil Kumar Yadav
Start Ur day with pure thoughts,

warm mind & kind heart.
Wakil Kumar Yadav
A sun is a beautiful reminder that
we can rise again from the darkness
that we have the power to shine
from within.
-Wakil Kumar Yadav
Sometimes u have to forget what's
gone, appreciate what still remains
& look forward to what's coming
next.
Wakil Kumar Yadav
Show respect even to those who
don't deserve it; not as a reflection
of their character, but as a reflection
of yours.
Wakil Kumar Yadav

Those who have nothing to offer for
the future keep harping on about
the past, cultures and traditions.
Wakil Kumar Yadav
If u persistently seek validation from
others, you will inadvertently
invalidate Ur own self-worth.
Wakil Kumar Yadav
Checking Ur phone for notifications
is just like opening Ur fridge more
than once when u knows there is no
food.

Wakil Kumar Yadav
Kindness has a beautiful way of
reaching down into a weary heart
and making it shine like the rising
sun.
Wakil Kumar Yadav
Distance doesn't necessarily to ruin
a relationship. U doesn't have to see
someone everyday to be in love.
-Wakil Kumar Yadav
Religious scriptures r the longest
"terms & conditions" that so many
people 'agree' to without knowing
why?
Wakil Kumar Yadav
Once u know the meaning of
"ACQUAINTANCE", u understand the
true meaning of frndship.
Wakil Kumar Yadav
Friendship is like a perennial river
which flows forever;
. It may change its path but will
never ever dry up...
Wakil Kumar Yadav
 friends are the most important
ingredient in this recipe of life....
Friendship Is Not a Game to Play,
It Is Not a Word to Say, It Doesn't

Start On March And Ends On May,
It Is Tomorrow, Yesterday, Today
and Every day.
Wakil Kumar Yadav
Kindness has a beautiful way of
reaching down into a weary heart
and making it shine like the rising
sun
Distance doesn't necessarily to ruin
a relationship. U don't have to see
someone everyday to be in love.
-Wakil Kumar Yadav
Religious scriptures r the longest
"terms & conditions" that so many
people 'agree' to without knowing
why?
Wakil Kumar Yadav
Some people may get a little upset if
their logic is challenged, but will
surely get very angry if their blind
faith is challenged.
Wakil Kumar Yadav
Crocodiles are fast on their feet,
but *cannot* turn very well. If one is
chasing you, run in zig zag lines.
Wakil Kumar Yadav

Our first impressions & reaction say
the most about the kind of person we
are.
--*Wakil Kumar Yadav*

  People say that money can't buy
love, but it can if u   .

--*Wakil Kumar Yadav*

The confidence level of a person can
be determined by whether their
actions are aimed at impressing
others, or inner satisfaction.

    --*Wakil Kumar Yadav*

We fear rejection, want attention,
crave affection, and dream of
perfection.
--*Wakil Kumar Yadav*

Ur hardest times often lead to the
greatest moments of Ur life. Keep
the faith. It will all be worth it in the
end.
    --*Wakil Kumar Yadav*

People usually forget to thank u
when u do well to them, but they
never forget to blame u if u did
wrong to them.

--Wakil Kumar Yadav

Make Ur happiness & personal
growth a priority in Ur life. The
more u take care of urself, the more
u can take care of others.

--Wakil Kumar Yadav

Sometimes u have to forget what's
gone, appreciate what still remains
& look forward to what's coming
next.

Wakil Kumar Yadav

Show respect even to those who
don't deserve it; not as a reflection
of their character, but as a reflection
of yours.

Wakil Kumar Yadav

Those who have nothing to offer for
the future keep harping on about
the past, cultures and traditions.

Wakil Kumar Yadav

If u persistently seek validation from
others, you will inadvertently
invalidate Ur own self-worth. *Wakil
Kumar Yadav*

Checking Ur phone for notifications
is just like opening Ur fridge more
than once when u know there is no
food.

Wakil Kumar Yadav

16

Everybody wants happiness, nobody
wants pain, but u can't have a
rainbow without a little rain.

**"It's okay to be angry.
It's never okay to be cruel."**
~ *Wakil Kumar Yadav*

**"Life is an echo.
What you send out comes back.
What you sow, you reap.
What you give, you get.
What you see in others exists in you.
Remember, life is an echo.
It always gets back to you.
So give goodness."**
~ *Wakil Kumar Yadav*

Waiting is linked to depression.
Time spent waiting for something
that may never happen can be
mentally painful.
--Wakil Kumar Yadav

Train Ur mind to see the good in
everything. Positivity is a choice.
-Wakil Kumar Yadav

17

The happiness of ur life depends on
the quality of ur thoughts.

Wakil Kumar Yadav

if u are looking for perfection, you'll
be looking forever.

Wakil Kumar Yadav

Do the things u enjoy the most &
hang out with the people u enjoy the
most.
Wakil Kumar Yadav

An ugly personality can easily
destroy a pretty face.

Wakil Kumar Yadav

Blowing out candles on birth day
cakes results in roughly 3000
bacteria capable of forming on the
cake.

-Wakil Kumar Yadav

Respect is earned. Honesty is
appreciated. Trust is gained. Loyalty
is returned.

- Wakil Kumar Yadav

That awkward moment when u

remember something funny can't
stop smiling like an idiot.

People are so quick to judge others
faults, but never quick to point out
their own.
Wakil Kumar Yadav

Hot water is more likely to break
thick glass than thin glass. That's
why test tubes are made of thin glass.

Wakil Kumar Yadav

Interrupted sleep is just as bad as a
night without sleep.
                    Wakil Kumar Yadav

"I choose freedom over a golden
cage; I choose the sky even if I sleep
on pavements"-

Wakil Kumar Yadav

Sometimes the bad things that
happen in our lives put as directly on
the path to the best things that will
ever happen to us.
Wakil Kumar Yadav

Forcing urself to forget something
causes the brain to think about it
even more.

Wakil Kumar Yadav

it's crazy how u can go months or
years without talking to someone but
they still across Ur mind every day.

Wakil Kumar Yadav

not being able to control Ur negative
thoughts is also a warning sign of
depression.
                Wakil Kumar Yadav

A positive attitude causes a chain
reaction of positive thoughts, events
& outcomes. It is a catalyst and it
sparks extraordinary results.

        Wakil Kumar Yadav

 A person generally hates for 3
reasons;
1) They want to be u...
2) they hate themselves.
3) They see u as a threat.
                Wakil Kumar Yadav

 If a single teacher can't teach us all
the subjects then how can u expect a
single student to learn all the
subjects?

Wakil Kumar Yadav

the true mark of maturity is when
somebody hurts u & u try to
understand their situation instead of
trying to hurt them back.
      Wakil Kumar Yadav

the most unimportant things you'll
ever need to know.
Ur body is as old as the Universe
bcoz matter never created or
destroyed.
      Wakil Kumar Yadav

Being in love show up in brain scans
like an addiction, not an emotion.

Wakil Kumar Yadav

A lot of probe alms in the world
would disappear if we talked to each
other instead of talking about each
other.
      Wakil Kumar Yadav

    Nothing in the world can
bother u, more than ur own
mind.

Wakil Kumar Yadav

"It's okay to be angry.
It's never okay to be cruel."
~ Wakil Kumar Yadav

"Life is an echo.
What you send out comes
back.
What you sow, you reap.
What you give, you get.
What you see in others
exists in you.
Remember, life is an echo.
It always gets back to you.
So give goodness."
~ Wakil Kumar Yadav

"One day it just clicks.
You realize
what's important and what isn't.
You learn to care less about
what other people think of you
and more about
what you think of yourself.
You realize how far you've come
and you remember
when you thought
things were such a mess
that you would never recover.
And you smile.
You smile because you are
truly proud of yourself

**and the person
you've fought to become."**
~ Wakil Kumar Yadav

**"Don't audit life.
Show up and make the
most of it now."**
~ Wakil Kumar Yadav

**"Arguing with an idiot is like
playing chess with a pigeon.
No matter how good you are,
the bird is going to poop on the
board
and strut around as if it won."**
~ Wakil Kumar Yadav

**"Worrying won't stop
the bad stuff from happening.
It just stops
you from enjoying the good."**
~ Wakil Kumar Yadav

Six ethics of life

Before you pray,
believe.
Before you speak,
listen.
Before you spend,
earn.
Before you write,
think.
Before you quit,
try.
Before you die,
live.
Wakil Kumar Yadav

Maybe you don't see people
looking at you
because you aren't looking at
them.
Maybe you don't hear all the
good things
people say about you
because you're too focused
on the bad.
Maybe you're a lot more
wonderful,
beautiful and special
than you give yourself credit
for."

24

Wakil Kumar Yadav

"Nobody can make you
happy
until you're happy with
yourself."
Wakil Kumar Yadav

Be an example...
show kindness to unkind
people.
Forgive people who don't
deserve it.
Love unconditionally.
Your actions always reflect
who you are."
~ *Wakil Kumar Yadav*

It's never too late to start over.
If you weren't happy with
yesterday
try something different today.

Don't stay stuck.
Do better."
Don't promise when you're happy.
Don't reply when you're angry,
and don't decide when you're sad.
" Don't ruin a new day
by thinking about yesterday.
Let it go."
~ *Wakil Kumar Yadav.*

Life & death are so unpredictable, so
close to each other. We exist
moment to moment, never knowing
who would be the next to leave the
world.
Wakil Kumar Yadav
Justice Dies when rapists are
supported
by the people.
Wakil Kumar Yadav
Even a tree that remains rooted in
one place eventually becomes a
landmark.
Wakil Kumar Yadav
Light always finds a way to shine.
Wakil Kumar Yadav
The pain which does not flow with
tears,

26

often found on paper with scatter
words.
Wakil Kumar Yadav
Although we may find comfort in
speech, silence may also have some
virtue.
Wakil Kumar Yadav
Promise is a big word.
It either makes something
or it breaks everything".
Wakil Kumar Yadav
Helping others is a nice way to help
you. *Wakil Kumar Yadav*
No summit of achievement is
attained in solo endeavors.
Wakil Kumar Yadav
Ask the soul
SOLITUDE IS AN ACHIEVEMENT.
Life does not need to be perfect to
be wonderful.
Wakil Kumar Yadav
The future belongs to those who
believe
in the beauty of their dreams.
Wakil Kumar Yadav
Curiosity is the most elegant
excuse for paying attention.
Wakil Kumar Yadav

A journey of a thousand memories
begins with a single step.
Wakil Kumar Yadav
CLARIFIES THE STEPS TO SIMPLIFY
THE JOURNEY.
Wakil Kumar Yadav
Ignoring the truth keeps you
in the shadows.
Wakil Kumar Yadav
Start Ur day with pure thoughts,
warm mind & kind heart.
Wakil Kumar Yadav
A sun is a beautiful reminder that
we can rise again from the darkness
that we have the power to shine
from within.
Wakil Kumar Yadav
Sometimes u have to forget what's
gone, appreciate what still remains
& look forward to what's coming
next.
Wakil Kumar Yadav
Show respect even to those who
don't deserve it; not as a reflection
of their character, but as a reflection
of yours.
Wakil Kumar Yadav
Those who have nothing to offer for

the future keep harping on about
the past, cultures and traditions.
Wakil Kumar Yadav
If u persistently seek validation from
others, you will inadvertently
invalidate Ur own self-worth.
Wakil Kumar Yadav
Checking Ur phone for notifications
is just like opening Ur fridge more
than once when u know there is no
food.
Wakil Kumar Yadav
Everybody wants happiness, nobody
wants pain, but u can't have a
rainbow without a little rain
Wakil Kumar Yadav
Some people may get a little upset if
their logic is challenged, but will
surely get very angry if their blind
faith is challenged.
Wakil Kumar Yadav
Crocodiles are fast on their feet, but
cannot turn very well. If one is
chasing you, run in zig zag lines.
Wakil Kumar Yadav
Kindness has a beautiful way of
reaching down into a weary heart
and making it shine like the rising

sun
Distance doesn't necessarily to ruin
a relationship. U don't have to see
someone everyday to be in love.
Wakil Kumar Yadav
Religious scriptures are the longest
terms & conditions that so many
people 'agree' to without knowing
why?
Wakil Kumar Yadav
Once u know the meaning of
"ACQUAINTANCE", u understand the
true meaning of frndship.
Wakil Kumar Yadav
Friendship is like a perennial river
which flows forever.
. It may change its path but will
never ever dry up...
Wakil Kumar Yadav

friends are the most important
ingredient in this recipe of life....
Friendship Is Not a Game to Play,
It Is Not a Word to Say, It Doesn't
Start On March And Ends On May,
It Is Tomorrow, Yesterday, Today
and Every day.
Wakil Kumar Yadav

Printed in Great Britain
by Amazon